CHINESE
FOOD AND DRINK

Amy Shui and Stuart Thompson

The Bookwright Press
New York · 1987

FOOD AND DRINK

Chinese Food and Drink
French Food and Drink
Indian Food and Drink
Italian Food and Drink

First published in the
United States in 1987 by
The Bookwright Press
387 Park Avenue South
New York, NY 10016

First published in 1987 by
Wayland (Publishers) Limited
61 Western Road, Hove
East Sussex BN3 1JD, England

ISBN 0–531–18129–4
Library of Congress Catalog Card Number:
86–73005

Typeset by DP Press, Sevenoaks
Printed in Italy by G. Canale & C.S.p.A., Turin

Cover *Although this book chiefly discusses the food and drink of the majority Han Chinese, it should not be forgotten that there are over fifty national minorities who have their own languages, customs, religions and styles of cooking and eating. The national minority people in this picture live in Kashgar in the west of China.*

Contents

China and its people 4
Food in China's past 9
Producing food 11
Processing and preserving food 15
Selling the food 18
Family meals 20
Chinese regional cuisine 23
Health and tradition 29
Kitchen and cooking equipment 31
Eating out 33
Drinks 37
Food for festive occasions 39
Chinese food abroad 41
Safety precautions and hints 44
Pronunciation guide 44
Using chopsticks 44
Glossary 46
Further reading 47
Index 48

China and its people

China is the most populated nation on earth. More than one billion people live there — about equal to the combined populations of Europe, the United States and the U.S.S.R. Of all world's people, more than one in every five is Chinese.

With an area of almost ten million square km (3.8 million sq mi), China is a huge country. Only the U.S.S.R. and Canada are bigger. But only about one-eighth of China's land is suitable for growing food. The rest is too mountainous, too desertlike, too cold or too dry. In China 22 percent of the earth's population gets its food from only 7 percent of the earth's cultivated land.

There are big differences in geography and climate from one part of China to another. To make things simpler, we can talk about two divisions (east and west; north and south) and three rivers.

The first important division is between the western and eastern halves of China. Generally, China slopes from high mountainous land in the west to lowlands in the east. In the southwest, Tibet (called "the roof of the world") is 4,000 m (13,200 ft) above sea level. In the northwest, erosion has been severe, and much of the area, including the vast region of Xinjiang, is desertlike.

Eastern China is much more suitable for agriculture, although even here many areas are too mountainous for farming. From the west, three major rivers twist and flow across the eastern half of China, creating fertile plains and basins along their route to the Pacific. The Yellow River got its name from the massive amount of fertile *loess* (yellow earth) which it has deposited in the wheat-growing North China Plain. Flowing through central China, the Yangtze River is 5,528 km (3,317 mi) long, the fourth largest river in the world. Farther south, the Xi River flows into the Pearl River Delta near Canton and Hong Kong.

The second important division is between north and south, particularly in eastern China. The dividing line is the Qinling mountain range, which lies between the Yellow and the Yangtze rivers. North of the Qinling Mountains, winters can be extremely cold, rainfall is unreliable, and wheat is the main crop. South of the Qinling mountains, winters are mild, rainfall plentiful and dependable, and the soil retains water well, so that rice grows well. Wheat is the staple food for north China and rice the staple food for the south.

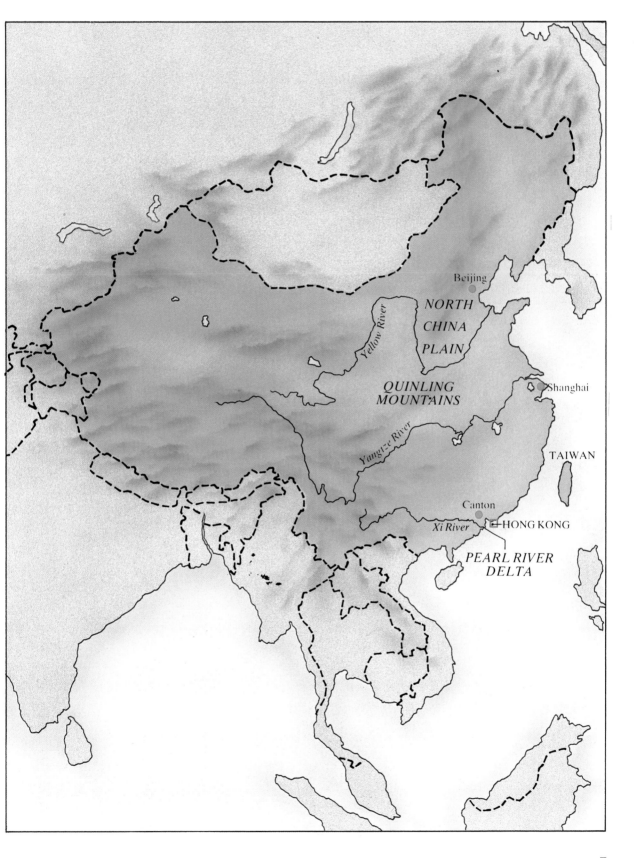

Beijing

NORTH
CHINA
PLAIN

Yellow River

QUINLING
MOUNTAINS

Shanghai

Yangtze River

TAIWAN

Canton

Xi River

HONG KONG

PEARL RIVER
DELTA

The Mongols, pictured here, are a nomadic, minority group who live in Inner Mongolia.

Not all people who live in the People's Republic of China (PRC) are Chinese, and not all Chinese people live in the PRC. Five million Chinese live in the British colony of Hong Kong, and eighteen million Chinese live under the flag of the Republic of China (ROC) on the island of Taiwan. In the last 150 years, millions of Chinese people have started new lives in other parts of the world, including Australia, New Zealand, the United States, Canada and Europe.

In China (PRC) there are more than fifty national minorities, peoples whose speech and traditions are not Chinese. Altogether there are about seventy million non-Chinese people in China. They have their own languages, customs, religions and styles of cooking and eating. Many (but not all) minority peoples live in the western half of China, which is very sparsely populated.

In contrast, eastern China is very densely populated. Almost nineteen out of every twenty people in China live in the eastern half. Eastern China has more than twenty cities with populations of over a million. The capital, Beijing, has a population of nine million, and the big industrial port of Shanghai has over twelve million. Although 200 million Chinese live in cities, four times as many Chinese are peasants who depend on agriculture for their livelihood.

China is divided into twenty-two provinces. Sichuan province's population of 100 million is greater than that of any country in Western Europe. Although written Chinese is the same all over China, spoken Chinese has several variations. Often the variety of Chinese spoken in one province cannot be understood in a neighboring province. Not surprisingly, cooking styles, also, vary a great deal among different provinces.

Chinese civilization can be traced back 4,000 years. The heart of this long-lasting civilization has always been in the eastern part of China. The size of the Chinese empire at times grew very large; at other times emperors were overthrown by foreign invaders, most notably the Mongols in the thirteenth century and the Manchus in the

A map showing the twenty-two provinces including Taiwan, (yellow) and the four autonomous regions of China (orange).

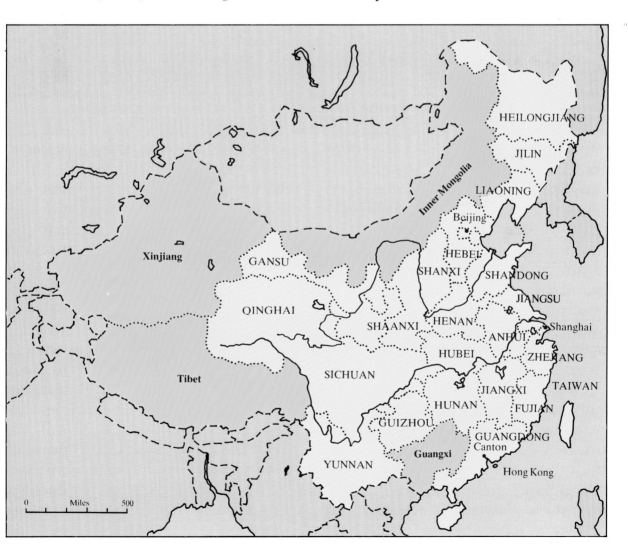

Mao Zedong's portrait above the entrance to "the Forbidden City" in Beijing. Mao Ze dong founded the People's Republic of China in 1949.

seventeenth century. But even with foreign emperors, Chinese civilization was not crushed.

By the nineteenth century, however, the greed and military strength of the Western nations had become threatening. China, once the most advanced nation on earth, was weak by comparison. One humiliation followed another and the ordinary Chinese suffered greatly. There were rebellions, civil wars, and foreign invasions. The Taiping rebellion in the mid-nineteenth century cost more lives than were lost on all sides in the First World War.

The last emperor gave up his throne in 1912, but civil wars, chaos and famines continued through the 1920s and became worse in the 1930s when the Japanese invaded China. After Japan's defeat in World War II, Mao Zedong and the Communists battled with Chiang Kai-shek's Nationalist followers for control of China. Mao won, and, in 1949, proclaimed China the "People's Republic of China." Chiang Kai-shek escaped with many of his soldiers to Taiwan. There he set up the rival "Republic of China" government-in-exile.

Food in China's past

Throughout their long history, the Chinese have always cherished their food. Early written records describe elaborate sacrifices and food offerings to the dead. They also tell how, in the times of the Shang dynasty (around 1750–1220 B.C.), more than 2,000 people were responsible just for preparing and serving meals in the royal palace! At that time they were already using bowls and chopsticks.

A 2,000-year-old tomb excavated in 1974 at Mawangdui gives us a lot of information. Pots and baskets of food, and even recipes inscribed on bamboo slips, were buried with the dead woman. Most of the cooking techniques and utensils used then are still used today. As the Chinese empire expanded, new foodstuffs entered China from Central Asia. In northern China Muslim influence can be seen in the form of dumplings and *wonton* (see p.36) and a liking for mutton and goat meat rather than pork.

During the Tang (A.D. 618–907) and Song (A.D. 960–1279) dynasties, China could boast the greatest and most commercial cities in the world. Especially during the Song dynasty, with its southern capital at Hangzhou, Chinese cuisine really blossomed. In the thirteenth century the traveler Marco Polo marveled at the huge open-air markets there, and the vast variety of restaurants and cuisines which

Detail from a late tenth-century painting entitled "Han Xizai's Evening Party."

The nutritional value of rice – which these people are transplanting – is very high, and its cultivation is widespread throughout China.

far surpassed those of his native Venice, the most developed city in Europe at that time.

From the sixteenth century onward, European nations traded by sea with China. They were attracted by China's silk, porcelain, tea and handicrafts. In return, vegetables such as sweet potatoes, white potatoes, corn and peanuts were introduced into China. These crops were nutritious, and could be grown on land unsuitable for rice.

European influence in the nineteenth century was much more harmful to China. The one major Western influence on the Chinese diet then was the introduction of opium by British merchants to pay for their exports of Chinese tea. Opium addiction became widespread in southern China.

In the latter half of the nineteenth and first part of the twentieth century, civil wars, foreign exploitation, population pressure and continuous turmoil resulted in much hardship and starvation. In China's long history, however, famines following floods or droughts have been common, and millions have died from hunger. China's poor developed a rich knowledge of famine foods to help them survive in desperate circumstances. At the other extreme, China's scholarly elite prided themselves on their knowledge of *haute cuisine*. A Chinese proverb states that "a banquet in a rich family could feed a poor man for half a year."

Producing food

When Mao Zedong and the Communist Party established the People's Republic of China in 1949 their most pressing problem was to eliminate hunger and the threat of hunger. They gave top priority to the task of ensuring that China's population was adequately fed.

The Chinese Communist Party introduced various measures toward achieving this. First, the ownership of land was changed. Land was taken from the rich and given to those with little or no land.

Then, during the 1950s, groups of peasant households were urged or forced to collectivize, that is, to combine their land and farm equipment and to farm together cooperating as a team. The idea was that it would be much more efficient for farmers to work together as members of big cooperatives, instead of each

Under the collective system, groups of peasant households worked together. This picture shows such a cooperative harvesting.

People are encouraged to produce their own food in China today. Here children in kindergarten are learning how to grow lettuce.

concerning himself with his own small farm. Big and important projects, such as building irrigation systems, would be easier with people working together in co-operation.

Under this collective system, many large-scale projects were carried out. Most important, the amount of irrigated land was increased from 20 to 45 million hectares (49 to 111 millions acres). Food production increased from year to year, especially grain production. Needy households were guaranteed an adequate food supply. The problem of feeding the

people seemed to been solved.

Mao Zedong died in 1976, and his successor, Deng Ziaoping, has been less convinced of the benefits of collectivization, believing that people work much harder when they work for themselves. Since 1979 a series of reforms have dismantled the collectives, and, as in the past, each household is responsible for what it does with its own section of land. Under the collective system, most produce had to be sold to the state. Now the peasant household has the incentive of being able to sell its produce in the rural markets which are flourishing again.

Growing enough food for China's huge population is not easy when so little of the land is suitable for agriculture. The farmland that is available has to be used very efficiently to supply China's people with enough food.

Growing grains, especially rice and wheat, is the most efficient way to use land, because they give more calories per acre than other crops. Altogether, more than 80 percent of China's cultivated land is used for growing grain. The average Chinese family gets more than three-quarters of its food energy from *fan* (cooked grains). The 1984 grain harvest was a record at over 400 million ton.

North of the Qinling mountain range, wheat is the main crop; although in some regions millet, corn and sorghum, or kaoliang, are grown. In southern China rice is the most important crop. The Chinese like to grow rice whenever water and soil permit, and they consider it to be the supreme food, the "Oriental staff of life."

With irrigation and adequate fertilizer it is possible in fertile areas, such as southeastern China, to have two rice crops and a winter crop on the same land each year. Such "multi-cropping" obviously makes much more efficient use of farmland. About half of China's cultivated land is irrigated, but two-thirds of China's grain comes from such land. This means that, on the whole, irrigated land produces double the amount of produce that nonirrigated land does.

Pork is the favorite meat of the Chinese. Most peasant households keep a pig, fed largely on household scraps. A pig is an investment. When the family needs

A peasant family's most important possession is a pig. A pig is seen as an investment since it is cheap to raise, provides manure and, if necessary, can be sold at market.

money they will sell the pig for cash. It is like a "piggy bank"! Another reason for keeping a pig is that it provides manure for the fields. Mao Zedong described the pig as "a walking fertilizer factory." Peasant households usually keep a few hens or ducks as well.

In the coastal provinces, such as Guangdong and Fujian, seafood is an important part of the diet. Besides salt-water fish, the Chinese near the coast eat clams, squid, shrimp, oysters, crabs and lobsters. In addition, China has thousands of rivers, lakes and ponds, and the Chinese have been raising fish for 3,000 years in these inland waters. Nowadays over 800 varieties of fish are farmed, carp being the most common. China produces more

With so many inland waterways, fish farming is an important activity.

freshwater fish than any other country. Fish farming (or aquaculture) is the most efficient way to produce animal protein.

Vegetables are a vital part of the low-meat Chinese diet, for they provide most of the nutrients missing from rice or wheat. Soy beans are particularly nutritious, and, in one form or another, are consumed throughout China. North and northeastern China are the main areas for soy bean production. Altogether there are about 120 types of vegetables grown in China. About half of these have been introduced from abroad. Vegetables are usually grown by peasants in garden-size plots near their homes. More vegetables can be grown in the south of China than in the north, where the harsh winters mean that the growing season is short.

Southern China also produces a greater variety of fruits including melons, bananas, kumquats, lychees, mangoes, peaches, pineapples, tangerines, as well as several fruits little known in the West.

China is the world's second-largest producer of tea, which is grown mainly in the hills of the southeast and central China. Sugar cane and peanuts (for cooking oil) are also important. Of the nonfood products that are grown, the most important are cotton, mulberry bushes (for silkworms) and tobacco.

Processing and preserving food

Preserving allows food to be stored for eating out-of-season, or to be transported to areas where the food is not produced.

The soy bean is extremely rich in protein and cheap to grow. Pound for pound it contains twice as much protein as steak. However, soy beans have to be processed, for otherwise they are indigestible. The Chinese have developed many food products that are based on the soy bean.

Best known is soy sauce, which is essential for Chinese cooking. Soy beans can also be soaked, crushed and strained to produce soy bean milk. Bean curd (*tofu*) is a whitish color, semi-solid in texture, neutral in taste, and very nutritious. It mixes well with other ingredients (see *Ma Po* recipe below). Bean-curd skin is called "the meat without bones" for it can be used to make imitiation meat. In addition, there are many pastes, sauces, and relishes that have processed soy bean as their base. The soy bean is the "king" of processed Chinese foods, and many of its products take the place of dairy products, such as milk and cheese, which Chinese people dislike.

Soy beans are used a great deal in Chinese cooking. Here a girl is eating bean curd, one of the products based on soy beans.

Pickled cabbages and turnips, and other preserved vegetables, are particularly important in north China where the winters prevent the growing of fresh vegetables.

Dried or salted fish give essential

"Thousand-year-old eggs" are preserved eggs that have a dark-green yolk and are considered a delicacy by the Chinese.

protein to those who cannot afford fresh meat or fish. Shellfish, too, can be dried or salted, but are more likely to be made into strong-tasting sauces and pastes, such as oyster sauce and shrimp paste.

Meats are preserved in many different ways. For example, there are Chinese sausages that taste vaguely like salami. Yunnan ham is something like our smoked bacon. Nanjing duck is boned, flattened under a heavy weight, and then finally cured.

Eggs, too, are preserved in various ways. The well known "thousand-year-old eggs" are an exaggeration. The eggs are more likely to be less than a hundred days old. They are covered with a lime-clay-hay mixture which causes a chemical reaction. When unwrapped, the egg white will have become rubbery in texture, and dark amber in color; the yolk will be cheesy in texture, and green in color. The taste is unusual and not to everyone's liking!

Ma Po's bean curd (Western cuisine)

You will need:

4 squares of bean curd (*tofu*)
2 teaspoons ginger, chopped
125 g (4 oz) ground pork or beef
2 tablespoons soy sauce
1 teaspoon cornstarch
2 cloves garlic, chopped
2 scallions (green onions), chopped
200 ml (¾ cup) water
2 tablespoons oil
½–1 tablespoon chili bean paste
(depending on how hot you want it)

What to do:

(1) Cut the bean curd into smaller cubes and chop the ginger, scallions, and garlic. Mix the water with the chili bean paste and soy sauce. (2) In a pan or *wok* heat the oil and fry the ginger, scallion and garlic for 20 seconds. Add the ground pork/beef and mix together. Keep stirring for 2 minutes. (3) Now add the chili bean paste, water, soy sauce and bean curd. Bring to the boil and turn the heat down. Simmer for about 3 minutes. Spoon some of the sauce into a bowl and mix with the cornstarch. Pour the cornstarch mix onto the bean curd and meat and stir. (4) When the sauce has thickened, turn off the heat and serve.

17

Selling the food

On the average, Chinese families in the People's Republic of China (PRC) spend three-fifths of their income on food. With that sort of outlay, shopping is an important skill. Two hundred years ago, the gourmet, Yuan Mei, reckoned that 60 percent of the credit for a good meal should be due to the cook, and the other 40 percent should go to the buyer of the ingredients. This idea has not changed much.

Chinese housewives like to buy food fresh from the market every day. Items are on open display, and seldom packaged or processed. Chickens are often sold live, so you can be sure of their freshness!

Chinese cooking requires fresh ingredients. There are very few convenience foods, although some produce markets and street stalls now sell chopped-up vegetables and meat, which just need to be quickly stir-fried to be ready to eat with rice or noodles. The Chinese do not buy frozen foods, and regard canned foods as a last resort. Village or neighborhood stores sell everyday provisions such as soy sauce, sugar, oil, cigarettes, soft drinks and some canned or preserved foods.

Stores such as this one sell basic provisions as well as canned and preserved fruit.

Up until the late 1970s, the state controlled the buying and selling of food. The state decided what the farm collectives should grow, and the collectives had to sell their produce to the state, which then sold to the public through state-run stores and markets. Key foods like rice, flour, cooking oil, meat, sugar and eggs were rationed. In this way the state was able to control food production, prices and distribution to ensure that basic foodstuffs were distributed fairly and equally. But supplies of nonbasic foodstuffs were often scarce, and many foods were just not available for much of the time.

The 1980s have seen changes. Collective land has been parceled

Since the beginning of the 1980s, people have been encouraged to sell their own produce in the markets.

out to individual households, which can now choose what to grow. Peasants can now sell their produce at open markets which have sprung up by the thousands around the country. So peasants who live in the areas around large towns and cities transport (often overnight, by bicycle or push-cart) their fresh vegetables or meat to sell on the open market. Although prices are dearer than in the state-run markets, people like the greater choice of products available, and the shorter lines.

Family meals

Eating is always something that the Chinese look forward to, and so cooking family meals is seen as a worthwhile activity. For women, however, it is also a time-consuming chore requiring them to spend up to three or four hours a day in the kitchen. One rule about family meals is that they should always be frugal.

A Chinese meal consists of two parts: the *fan* (rice, or other cooked staple) and *cai* (accompanying vegetable and/or meat dishes). Of the two, the *fan* part is the more important, for a meal is not thought to be a meal if there is no *fan*. The *cai* is there merely to flavor the rice.

Midday and evening meals are much the same, although a family is more likely to be able to eat together in the evening. Ideally a family meal should consist of the *fan*, three or four *cai* dishes, and one or two soups. To give variety and balance

A balance of cai *and* fan *is important at every family meal.*

to the meal, the *cai* should include a dish containing meat (pork or poultry), a dish with fish or seafood, and a fresh vegetable dish. Many rural families cannot afford such variety except on special occasions, and they rely on cheaper *cai* such as salted fish, bean curd or pickled vegetables. Many families eat meat less than once a week.

Each diner has a pair of chopsticks, a bowl, a flat-bottomed spoon (for soup) and, perhaps, a saucer. Rice is served from the common pot to each person's bowl – it is very difficult to eat rice from a plate using chopsticks. The *cai* dishes and the soups are placed together at the center of the table within everyone's reach. There is no main course, and no dessert. Soup is taken almost as a beverage. Since the *cai* have already been cut into bite-sized pieces, knives are not needed; indeed, it seems wrong to see a knife on the dinner table.

Throughout the meal each person uses chopsticks to transfer mouthfuls of *cai* to his or her rice bowl. It is bad-mannered to pile *cai* on one's rice. The fact that family members are sharing *cai* from common dishes is thought to help create a feeling of family togetherness.

Since a family meal is a communal activity, an occasion for family harmony and unity, it is very wrong to express anger at the table. It is good manners to eat more *fan* than *cai*, and others at the table

It is quite acceptable to lift your bowl and "shovel" food into your mouth.

should not be able to tell which *cai* is your favourite. It is rude to bite or suck your chopsticks, and even worse to delve through the *cai* in an attempt to find "a good bit." Although it is quite acceptable to lift one's bowl and "shovel" the contents into one's mouth with chopsticks, it is wrong to hold the bowl in one's palm for that is the action of a beggar. It is impolite not to finish every grain of rice in your bowl, for it is remembered that each grain was produced only by the hard work of the farmer.

Noodles with meat sauce (Northern cuisine)

Not all Chinese families have rice as their staple food, especially in the north, where wheat is more common. Here is a sample northern dish, with wheat noodles rather than rice:

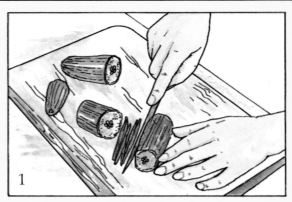

What you need:
500 g (1 lb) ground pork or beef
500 g (1 lb) noodles or spaghetti
3 tablespoons yellow bean paste
1 tablespoon sherry
1 teaspoon sesame oil
3 tablespoons peanut or vegetable oil
4 large cloves of garlic, finely chopped
1 tablespoon soy sauce
1 teaspoon sugar
1 cucumber
60 ml (¼ cup) water

What to do:
(1) Cut the cucumber into 4 sections and shred each section to get thin strips of cucumber. Set aside on a plate. Heat up the *wok* or frying pan and add the oil. (2) When the oil is hot, add the garlic. Fry for half a minute until the aroma breaks out then add the pork or beef. Stir-fry until cooked. Add the sherry, soy sauce, yellow bean paste, sugar and water. Simmer until the meat sauce thickens. (3) Boil the water and cook the noodles or spaghetti in the boiling water until done and then drain. Mix the noodles with the sesame oil. (4) Serve the noodles in individual bowls and top with meat sauce. To eat: mix the noodles with the meat sauce. Eat with the cold cucumber, which serves as a refreshing contrast to the salty meat sauce.

Chinese regional cuisines

Within Chinese cuisine there is a vast range of styles and local specialties. For convenience we can divide Chinese cuisine into four main regions or "schools": East, South, West and North.

The Eastern (or Shanghai) School

Shanghai is the biggest and most important city in this region. Rich soil and a good irrigation system around the Yangtze River means that the land here is very fertile. Rice is the main crop but wheat is grown in the north of the region. The favorable climate means that vegetables and fresh fruits grow very well. The region is famous for its vegetarian dishes. The long coastline provides a variety of seafood, and the many inland lakes and rivers provide a ready supply of freshwater fish.

The cooking of this region is very varied and includes stir-frying, red-stewing (simmering in soy sauce) and steaming. People here like to add sugar to their recipes.

Southern (or Cantonese) School

In this region, a climate of mild winters and plentiful rainfall, combined with fertile land, especially around the Pearl River Delta, mean that a huge variety of excellent fruits (including oranges,

Shanghai is China's busiest port.

23

Cabbage with cream sauce (Eastern cuisine)

You will need:
750 g (1½ lb) Chinese cabbage
15 g (½ oz) ham
½ teaspoon sugar
3 tablespoons oil
½ teaspoon salt

cream sauce:
100 ml (½ cup) milk
220 ml (1 cup) chicken stock or water
2 teaspoons cornstarch
1 teaspoon salt

What to do:
Separate the cabbage leaves from the stalk. Wash and dry the cabbage leaves. (1) Cut the leaves crosswise into about 3 sections (the leaf part can be wider). Shred the ham. In a bowl, mix together the stock or water, milk, salt and cornstarch. Heat a *wok* or frying pan, then add the oil. (2) Add the cabbage leaves and stir-fry for about 2 minutes. Add the salt and sugar and continue to stir-fry for another minute. (3) Remove the cabbage to a plate. Bring the cream sauce to the boil in the wok or frying pan. Turn the heat down. Add the cabbage and ham and mix with the sauce. Remove the cabbage with a slotted spatula to a plate. (4) Pour the remaining sauce over the cabbage and serve immediately.

pineapples and lychees) and vegetables can always be found as fresh ingredients. Rice can be harvested three times a year in many districts. Pork and poultry are the main meats, and the seafood is excellent.

In Cantonese cuisine, as in others, ingredients should be as fresh as possible. In cooking, the aim is to make sure that the natural flavor, texture and color of each ingredient remain unchanged as much as possible. Steaming is one way of achieving this, especially with fish. Stir-frying, which the Cantonese invented, is another. The Cantonese tend to avoid lengthier forms of cooking, partly to save fuel. They do not use a lot of oil or strong spices and prefer sauces that compliment rather than disguise the natural flavor of ingredients. Cantonese cuisine is probably an example of Chinese food at its very best.

Poultry is an important part of the Southern School's cuisine. This is a picture of a duck farm in the Pearl River Delta.

Stir-fry chicken with vegetables (Southern cuisine)

You will need:
2 breasts of chicken or 250g (½ lb) pork
  fillet
1 teaspoon salt
1 teaspoon sherry
1 egg white
1 teaspoon cornstarch
2 cloves of garlic
6 tablespoons oil
1 green pepper or 2 carrots or 2 zuccini
  or 250 g (½ lb) sweet corn or whatever
  vegetables you like

What to do:
Wash, peel and dice or slice the vegetables. (For stir-frying, dice into small ¾-inch cubes). Dice or slice meat. (If you have diced the vegetables, dice the meat. If you have sliced them, slice the meat.) Put the meat into a bowl and marinate with the salt, sherry, egg white and cornstarch.

Heat the frying pan or *wok* then pour in the oil to heat. Stir-fry the meat in hot oil for about 2 minutes. Using a metal slotted spoon, remove the meat to a dish. Pour off most of the oil and put to one side – it can be reused later. Using the remaining oil, stir-fry the vegetables and garlic for 2–3 minutes, depending on size and thickness. Do not overcook the vegetables. They should still be a little crunchy in texture. Combine the meat with the vegetables and stir-fry for another minute. Stir-fry chicken is best served with boiled rice.

Twice-cooked pork (Western cuisine)

You will need:

250 g (½ lb) boneless pork
1 green pepper
1 red pepper (optional)
1 onion
2 slices fresh ginger root
1 scallion (green onion)
2 cloves garlic (crushed)

sauce:
*½–1 tablespoon chili bean sauce
2 tablespoons water
4 tablespoons oil
½ teaspoon sugar
½ teaspoon salt
1 tablespoon Chinese barbecue sauce
   or black soy or hoinsin sauce
*(depending on how hot you want the sauce)

What to do:

(1) Boil the pork whole with the ginger and scallion in water for 20 minutes. Wash and de-seed the peppers. Cut the peppers into ½-in squares. Remove the pork from the pan and let it cool. (2) When cool, slice the pork thinly into squares roughly the same size as the peppers. (Save the stock for use as soup, e.g. in *wonton* soup.) Heat *wok* (or frying pan) and add the oil. (3) When oil is hot, stir-fry the meat with the garlic for half a minute. Pour off most of the oil – keeping it for later use. With remaining oil, stir-fry the scallions and the pepper for a minute. (4) Now add the sauce ingredients and the pork, and mix everything together quickly, ready for serving.

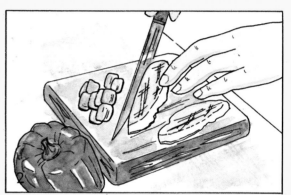

Western (or Sichuan) School

The Western region is all inland. Surrounded by mountains, it is quite isolated from the rest of China. This is reflected in its distinctive cuisine, which, unlike the rest of China's, is very spicy. The Yangtze flows through Sichuan, making this another of China's very fertile and populous areas. There are plenty of fruit and vegetables, and a great variety of peppers and chilis. Irrigation systems, which have existed for centuries, allow up to three rice crops per year. Again, animal protein is gained mostly from pork, poultry and freshwater fish.

Western cuisine is renowned for its chili-hotness. *Ma po's* bean curd and twice-cooked pork are both famous hot Sichuan dishes. Also famous is Sichuan duck smoked over tea leaves and chips of camphor wood, which is delicious!

Northern (or Beijing) School

The Northern School of Chinese cuisine is centered on the capital city of Beijing. In this northeastern part of the country winters are bitterly cold, while summers are hot and quite dry. The vast North

Peking Duck is best served with plum sauce and scallions in a pancake.

China Plain is flat and very fertile thanks to *loess* (yellow topsoil) carried by the Yellow River. It is a productive farming area with well-developed irrigation networks linked to the Yellow River.

The region is too cold, and the soil not suitable, for rice cultivation. Wheat, millet, barley and other cereals are cultivated instead. Flour is the basic staple in northern China, and is processed into a great variety of products – noodles, steamed breads and buns, pancakes, and dumplings of various sizes that have a variety of fillings.

Mongolian and Muslim influences have heavily affected Beijing cuisine. Mutton and goat meat are often preferred to pork, the favorite meat elsewhere in China. Northern cuisine tends to use strongly flavored seasonings such as vinegar, garlic, coriander, scallions, leeks and sesame oil.

Nowadays Beijing is best known abroad for its "Peking duck." The ducks, which have been fattened by force-feeding, are glazed and roasted. Slivers of the duck skin and meat are then sliced off, to be wrapped with a plum sauce or hoisin sauce and scallions in a light thin pancake for eating.

"Lion-heads" casserole (Northern cuisine)

You will need:
500 g (1 lb) ground pork
500 g (1 lb) Chinese cabbage
6 tablespoons oil
2 tablespoons water

paste:
1 teaspoon cornstarch
1 tablespoon water

mixing sauce:
1 egg
1 tablespoon sherry
1 teaspoon cornstarch
2 scallions (green onions)
1 teaspoon grated fresh ginger root
1 teaspoon salt
1 teaspoon sesame oil

What to do:
Separate, then wash cabbage leaves. Cut in 2, crosswise. Chop scallions fine, and grate the ginger. Combine ground pork with mixing sauce. Mix together well. Divide into 4 meatballs. Toss each meatball from one hand to another, back and forth, to draw out any air and make the meatballs firmer. Mix the cornstarch and water to make a paste in a small container.

Heat the frying pan or *wok*. Add the oil. Coat the meatballs all over with the paste. Brown the meatballs all over in the hot oil. Remove with a slotted spoon and put to one side. Pour off most of the oil, reserving it for later use. With the remaining oil, stir-fry the cabbage leaves for 2 minutes. Remove, and use them to line the bottom of a casserole pot. Put the meatballs on top of the leaves in the casserole. Add 2 tablespoons water. Cover with a lid and simmer for one hour on low heat. (Make sure the liquid does not dry up during cooking.)

Health and tradition

For centuries the Chinese have been aware that there is a close link between what you eat and your state of health. Everything you eat and drink has an effect on your body's *qi* (pronounced "chee" as in "cheese") meaning "vital energies." Illness is thought to occur when the body's *qi* are imbalanced. When Chinese people are ill the first remedy they try is often a change of diet so as to restore the balance of the body's *qi*. If food fails as the cure, only then will they make use of traditional herbal cures, acupuncture or Western-style drugs.

Since the Tang dynasty (A.D. 618–907), if not before, foods have been classified according to whether they "heat" or "cool" the body's *qi*. Foods that are thought to be particularly "heating" include rich, oily foods, fatty meat, heavily spiced food, and strong alcohol. "Cooling" foods include bland or bitter-tasting foods, most kinds of

Assistants dispensing traditional herbal medicine at a pharmacy.

vegetables, watery or citrus fruits, and nongreasy soups. Other foods, including rice, are "neutral" – that is, they neither "heat" nor "cool" the *qi*.

Eating too much "heating" food can result in the *qi*'s becoming too "hot" – a hangover is a good example of a "hot" illness! The remedy is to restore the balance by eating "cooling" foods, and avoiding "heating" foods until better. If the *qi* is too "cold," then you are likely to feel rather anemic and lacking in energy. To return to health, you should have more "heating" foods.

If you meet a Chinese friend, instead of "Hello!" you would probably be greeted with "Have you eaten?" This is the standard Chinese greeting. They suppose that if you have just eaten (which is the conventional reply, whether you have or not!), then you must be feeling fine.

Indeed, food is a sign of prosperity and good times. "Having grains to chew" is a Chinese way of saying that you have a job. A job in which you have a secure income is called "having an iron rice bowl" (i.e., it cannot be broken). "Having a porcelain rice bowl" means you have an insecure job, while "the rice bowl is broken" means you are unemployed.

When visiting friends and relatives it is common to take an item of food as a gift. Often foods can convey good wishes. Noodles, for example, because of their length, stand for "long life," and so are an apt birthday gift. The word for "cake" (*gao*) sounds the same as the word for "high," and so it symbolizes success.

At weddings a small child offers the bride a tangerine – the word for which, *ji*, puns with a word meaning "lucky." Many gifts given to newlyweds convey the hope that they will soon have children. On the other hand, the couple should not share (*fen*) a pear (*li*) because *fen-li* means "separation."

Noodles, seen here being sold at a street stand, are given as a gift to symbolize long life.

Kitchen and cooking equipment

The stove is an important symbol for the family in China. A family is said to be "people who share the same stove." In traditional China, an image of a Stove God was placed on a small altar just above the family stove. The Stove God's job was not to teach cooking, but, at the end of the year, to make a report to Heaven on how well the family had behaved.

Different regions of China have different types of stoves (depending on what sort of fuel is available). In the past, stoves were mostly big structures built of brick. They would have two openings at the top, one for cooking *fan* (the staple), and the other for cooking *cai* (accompanying dishes). These are beginning to be replaced by lightweight, two-burner, gas-fueled cook-tops. Another recent innovation is the electric rice boiler, which cooks rice automatically.

Chinese cooking utensils are few in number, but efficient, versatile, long-lasting and inexpensive. The undoubted star of the Chinese kitchen is the round-bottomed iron *wok*. Its rounded bottom means that less oil is needed; the *wok*'s depth makes rapid stirring and tossing easy; being made of iron it can take the intense heat needed for stir-frying and its curved shape allows heat to spread evenly over the *wok*.

Although superb for stir-frying, it is also useful for other cooking methods such as boiling, deep-frying and steaming.

The wide-bladed Chinese cleaver has many uses. It can be used for cutting meat as well as vegetables, and can do the job of chopping (through meat and bone), slicing, dicing and shredding. The flat of the blade can pound and crush ginger or garlic, as well as scoop ingredients off a chopping board.

This woman is using a cleaver, an implement that has a variety of uses in the Chinese kitchen.

Girls in a restaurant kitchen placing ingredients in bamboo steamers.

Cooking chopsticks are used for tasks such as lifting, whisking or mixing ingredients. Best made of bamboo, they are a few inches longer than dining chopsticks. Other tools for transferring or separating ingredients include a perforated spoon, a wire-mesh strainer, a metal spatula and ladle. These traditionally have long bamboo handles.

A lightweight earthenware cooking pot, called a "sandpot" (*sha guo*) may be used for slow-cooking processes, including "red-stewing." An ovenproof casserole dish or heavy iron cooking pot can be used instead. For steaming, a Chinese kitchen will have a set of bamboo steamers, and a metal or wooden rack. The bamboo steamers are piled on top of each other and set on the rack which stands over boiling water in the *wok*.

Eating out

Chinese people, especially those who live in towns and cities, do much of their eating away from home. There is a vast range of places at which to eat, from street hawkers pushing carts, to huge restaurants, such as the famous Peking Duck restaurant in Beijing which can seat 2,500 people at a time in over 40 dining rooms.

Many people "eat out" for breakfast, grabbing a bite to eat from a street stall on the way to work or school. At home a breakfast might consist of hot *congee* (thin rice porridge) with the evening meal's leftovers, or flavored with fermented bean curd, salted peanuts, pickled egg, or other preserved ingredients. From a street stall you might buy *you-tiao* ("oily stick"), a length of twisted dough, fried in oil, which tastes rather like a doughnut, washed down with hot soybean milk; or *man-tou* (steamed bread roll); or *bao-zi*, large steamed dumplings with various fillings; or turnip cake.

Many workers and students have lunch in large self-service cafeterias subsidized by their work unit or school. Others spend lunch-breaks eating at one of the small privately run food stalls or the restaurants, which began to appear in the 1980s after a period when they were banned. Each street vendor will specialize in two or three particular dishes or snacks only, providing a bench or two where customers can sit next to the cart or barrow. Food stalls, among them, sell a great variety of different foods, including all-in-one noodle dishes, one-bowl meals of rice and some kind of topping, dumplings by the dozen, many bean-curd specialties, hot sweet potatoes, barbecued meats, and eat-from-the-bag smoked duck. Other stalls specialize in providing drinks (like sugar cane and lemon juice) or sweet snacks, such as almond milk jelly (see below) or candied apples.

Especially in the Canton area, teahouses and restaurants often serve little snacks called *dim sum* (literally "dot the hearts," meaning

Food stands, such as this one, are convenient places for a snack and offer a variety of foods.

you "point to those that please the heart.") All in all there are probably more than a thousand different kinds of *dim sum*. They are usually spicy or salty, but may be sweet, and are usually steamed in bamboo baskets. In large *dim sum* restaurants, waitresses push trolleys loaded with various *dim sum* up and down the aisles between tables, allowing diners to choose at leisure.

The Chinese rarely invite guests to meals at home. They prefer to entertain by eating out. Ordinary restaurants in the PRC still tend to be rather dingy, with plastic tables, stark decorations, poor lighting, and menus chalked on a blackboard. Nonetheless, because of a shortage of restaurants, such places tend to be very crowded – and it is

the quality of the food rather than the surroundings that the Chinese are most concerned about.

Many of the bigger restaurants have two sections. One is for the majority of customers, and the other is for "privileged" persons, a category that includes foreigners (whether they want such special treatment or not), Chinese from overseas and officials in the Communist Party. Food at these restaurants is magnificent and, for those who can afford the prices, very exotic – one famous restaurant in Canton, for instance, specializes in snake-meat dishes.

Dim sum snacks generally require too much effort to be made at home, but the following *wonton*-based soup and dumplings are not too difficult. *Wonton* is Chinese ravioli or dumplings. The most popular way to serve *wonton* is in *wonton*

Just a few of the thousand varieties of dim sum

oup. Because of the softness of the skin, the Cantonese have called it "swallowing cloud" – which sounds the same as *wonton*. You can buy ready-made *wonton* skins from any Chinese foodstore.

The Chinese will usually entertain friends in a restaurant rather than at home.

One of the most popular sweet dishes available from street stands is Almond milk jelly.

Almond milk jelly (Southern cuisine)

You will need:

1 can of fruit cocktail (use assorted fresh fruit if preferred)
300 ml (1¼ cups) milk
300 ml (1¼ cups) water
1 package unflavored gelatine
1 teaspoon almond extract
3 tablespoons sugar
syrup from canned fruit or juice from fresh fruit

What to do:

Boil half the water and pour into a bowl for setting the jelly. Pour the gelatine powder over the hot water and stir until the powder has completely dissolved. Stir in the sugar. Add the rest of the water, the milk and the almond essence. Mix thoroughly. Put the bowl of almond mixture into the refrigerator and wait till it is completely set. If using fresh fruit, prepare and dice it. When the almond jelly is set, cut into cubes and divide it among the serving bowls. Top the jelly with fresh or canned fruit cocktail. Pour fruit syrup or juice over and serve.

Wonton soup (Southern cuisine)

You will need:
filling:
500 g (1 lb) ground pork
1 scallion (green onion)
½ teaspoon salt
1 teaspoon cornstarch
1 teaspoon dry sherry
1 teaspoon thin soy sauce
1 teaspoon sesame oil
20–24 *wonton* skins

soup:
500 ml (16 fl oz) chicken stock or broth
scallion, chopped
dash of sesame oil
4 lettuce leaves

What to do:
Chop the scallions. Mix filling ingredients together in a mixing bowl. (1) Scoop a small amount of filling and place in the middle of a *wonton* skin. (2) Fold the *wonton* by gathering the 4 corners together and pinching the wrapper together over the filling. Make sure the skin is sealed where you pinch it. The *wonton* should look like a small pouch.

Half fill a large saucepan with water. Bring water to boil. (3) Gently drop the *wonton* into the water. Wait till the *wonton* rise to the surface, then continue to boil for another 3 minutes. Remove the *wonton* and divide them equally among the soup bowls. Bring the stock to the boil. Tear lettuce leaves into halves. (4) Add the lettuce leaves, scallion and sesame oil to stock. Remove soup from the heat, pour over *wonton* in soup bowls. Serve hot.

Drinks

The Chinese were the first to discover tea as a drink. The English word "tea" comes from the Chinese. There are three main types of tea. "Green tea" is made from dried tea leaves. "Black tea" is the type popular in the West. For this the tea leaves are crushed and broken, and then left in damp, warm air to ferment. They turn from green to black, and acquire a stronger taste. The third type, *Oolong* ("Black Dragon") tea, is only partly fermented.

A girl harvesting tea. Different methods are used to produce three kinds of tea: Black tea, Green tea and Oolong.

Most Chinese avoid "black tea," which they regard as only fit for export to foreign lands where people add milk and sugar. In China, the only thing added to a mug or glass with tea leaves at the bottom is boiled water. For them the aroma of green or *Oolong* tea should be enjoyed in its own right.

Some types of tea are thought to have health-giving properties – to aid digestion, for instance. The very best brands of tea can be very expensive and in Taiwan and Fujian, the wealthier people drink very strong, bitter "Black Dragon" tea from thimble-sized cups.

Although China now grows some coffee, it has not yet become popular as a beverage. But Chinese people do not drink tea all the time.

Although beer has never been a traditional drink, there are now a number of breweries in China.

At meals, soup is more likely to be the only source of liquid. Western-style soft drinks are becoming popular, and, since 1981, China has marketed its own Cola drink – *Tian-fu Cola* is now being made in over 650 factories.

Alcoholic drinks have been made in China for some 3,500 years. There is some grape wine, but it is of poor quality. Better, and more popular, are the various vodkas distilled from different grains. Some are extremely strong. One of the most famous is *Mao Tai*, a vodka made from sorghum. Less lethal is the amber-colored *Shao Hsing*, made from glutinous rice, and a favorite at wedding banquets.

Alcohol is consumed only with food. A Chinese person who drinks alone will be frowned upon, for drinking is a social activity. At banquets a great deal of alcohol may be consumed. It is rude, though, to drink without toasting a fellow guest every time you lift your glass. The Chinese like to celebrate an event by holding a banquet at which there may be a minimum of ten or twelve dishes. Drinking games are an important part at these banquets, which can become quite noisy toward the end as some of the participants challenge each other to "guess-fingers" or other such drinking games.

Beer is not a traditional Chinese drink, but there are now more than 500 breweries in China. *Tsingtao* beer is the most famous variety.

Food for festive occasions

Most Chinese like nothing better than feasting! For them eating well is what makes a holiday festive. At times, the Communist government has criticized feasting as "wasteful" and "unproductive," but most Chinese enjoy a good meal too much to worry about criticism. All Chinese festivals provide an excuse for feasting, and many are associated with the eating of special foods.

The Chinese New Year Festival is a family occasion, the most important part being the sharing of the New Year's Eve dinner. Preparations start days before, and the atmosphere is busy and festive. In the north, family members often join together to wrap dozens of little mince-filled dumplings (jiao-zi). There will be much more meat than usual. Families that can afford it will have dishes that include pork, whole chicken and whole fish (fish is a symbol for plenty). Some foods, such as fish, are included because they have lucky associations. New Year Cake (nian-gao) is a favorite item (see below). It is sweet and gooey, being made into slabs from brown sugar and glutinous rice. Another popular item is tang-yuan, red or white marble-sized balls of glutinous rice flour, sometimes with a sesame filling. The term tang-yuan sounds like a term meaning "reunion," and thus is very apt. Family members should "stick together" the way the tang-yuan do! For several days after New Year's there is more feasting as friends and relatives visit each other.

At the mid-autumn Moon Festival, people sit outside and admire the Full Moon. In the past

Moon cakes on a street stand. These cakes are traditionally eaten at the mid-autumn Moon Festival.

The colorful Dragon Boat Festival in Hong Kong. The festival usually occurs between the end of May and the beginning of June.

everyday life, and included many rituals for offering food, incense and spirit money to the gods, ghosts and ancestors that were thought to live on in the world of the dead. Such rituals can be quite spectacular. For example, in northern Taiwan every few years households compete to see who can produce the biggest pig to offer to a local god. In the PRC, however, such rituals are frowned upon by the Communist Party as "superstitious practices," and are therefore restricted.

this was probably a harvest festival. Now people enjoy themselves eating moon cakes (round baked pastries with many different fillings), and various fruits shaped like the moon (melons, peaches, apples and pomegranates).

Another special festival food is *zong-zi*, which is eaten at the Dragon Boat Festival. *Zong-zi* are fist-sized parcels of glutinous rice wrapped in lotus leaves. Some have spicy meat fillings, while others contain sweet bean paste.

These and other festivals are celebrated throughout most of China. In addition many festivals are celebrated only in particular regions or villages. In traditional China, festivals were a more common and colorful feature of

Chinese New Year cake

You will need:
500 g (1 lb) brown sugar
500 g (1 lb) glutinous rice flour

What to do:
Boil 300 ml (1¼ cups) of water. Take from the heat, and add the sugar, mixing till it becomes syrupy. Pour the flour into a large bowl, and add the syrup a little at a time, stirring as you do so. Keep mixing until it becomes smooth. Grease a 20 cm (8 in) cake tin, and pour the mixture into it. Boil at least two pints of water in a large pot or *wok*. Carefully place the cake tin on a steaming-rack standing in the water. Cover the pot or *wok* with a lid and steam for 2 hours, making sure that the water does not boil dry.

The *nian-gao* (New Year Cake) will keep for weeks. In fact it tastes better the older it is. It can be resteamed to eat hot, or can be eaten cold as a sticky, sweet snack.

Chinese food abroad

There are estimated to be more than twenty-five million Chinese living overseas. From the 1840s onward, life was so harsh for many Chinese people that thousands braved leaving home to start new lives in distant lands. The majority settled in the countries of Southeast Asia, but many went much farther, to Latin America, Australia and especially the western coasts of the United States and Canada.

As Chinese emigrants settled around the world, so Chinese cuisine spread with them. Now Chinese restaurants can be found in most towns and cities in Canada and the United States, Western Europe and Australia. Most early settlers came from southern China, and so Chinese food abroad has

Grant Street, Chinatown, San Francisco. "Chinatowns" can now be found in several big cities outside China, particularly in North America, Australasia and Europe.

tended to be Cantonese style.

Often dishes have been adapted to suit the tastes of non-Chinese customers. *Chop suey* is a dish that originated in the United States, not China. Popular dishes such as *chow mein* ("fried noodles"), "sweet and sour pork" and "fried rice" (see below) have been adapted and have "caught on" because they are quickly cooked (by stir-frying) as well as being cheap. Hong Kong Chinese who came to the United States in the 1960s and early 1970s established thousands of restaurants or family-run "take-outs" that serve this adapted kind of Chinese cuisine.

To enjoy more authentic and delicious Chinese food, the best restaurants are to be found in the Chinatown districts of cities such as San Francisco, New York or London. Chinatown restaurants and grocery stores cater primarily to Chinese customers who appreciate and expect "the real thing." Cantonese cuisine is the dominant style, with Beijing-style next in popularity. The better restaurants are those in which most of the customers are Chinese. To enjoy as wide a variety of dishes as possible it is best to go in a group of six or more persons, for you should

With the growing interest in Chinese food abroad, Chinese grocery stores and supermarkets, like this one in London, have sprung up all over the world.

42

order as many dishes as there are people eating.

One of the easiest and quickest Chinese dishes is fried rice. It is a good way to use up leftover rice and any other cooked food. You can almost add any variety of ingredients you like.

Fried rice (Southern cuisine)

You will need:
2–4 eggs (minimum 2 eggs for 4 people)
2 scallions (green onions)
2 tablespoons oil
½ teaspoon salt
4 slices bacon or ham
60 g (2 oz) frozen shrimps (optional)
60 g (2 oz) frozen peas
sufficient boiled rice

What to do:
(1) Chop the scallions and dice the bacon or ham. Beat the eggs and add salt. Heat the frying pan or *wok*. Pour in 1 tablespoon oil. (2) When the oil is hot, pour in the beaten egg. Turn the egg once, as with an omelette. Remove the egg onto a side plate. (3) Add remaining oil and fry the meat. Add the frozen peas and shrimps and stir-fry for a few minutes. Turn the heat down. Add the cooked egg, and cut it into small bits. (4) Add the cooked boiled rice and the chopped scallions. Mix thoroughly. The fried rice is now ready to serve.

1

3

2

4

Appendix

Safety precautions and hints

1. Always wear an apron especially when frying food, because of the chance of oil splattering when ingredients are added to hot oil. Be very careful when adding ingredients to hot oil.
2. Do not use plastic implements when frying food as the heat of the oil may melt them.
3. Use a splatter shield or screen when cooking with oil to protect yourself. HOT OIL SCALDS AND BURNS.
4. When stir-frying meat, use more oil than is necessary. Make sure that enough hot oil is in contact with every bit of meat. Pour excess oil away when meat is cooked – the oil can be reused later. But BE CAREFUL!

Pronunciation guide

The Chinese do not use an alphabet or letters for writing, so, when English letters are used to represent Chinese words, the sounds of some letters are different from the usual English pronunciation. For instance:

C is pronounced like the "ts" sound in the word "cats"; so the word *cai* should be pronounced "tsai" (and rhyme with lie).

Xi sounds roughly like "she," and *Zinjiang* sounds roughly like "shin" + "jang" as in "jangle").

Q is pronounced rather like "ch," and so *Qinling* sounds like the word "chin" + "ling."

Zh sounds like "j," and so *Hangzhou* sounds rather like "hang Joe."

As you will realize from these examples, Chinese is often difficult for English-speakers to pronounce; but, then, English is an equally difficult language for Chinese-speakers to master.

Using chopsticks

Few things are more frustrating than not being able to transfer tasty Chinese food from bowl to mouth because you cannot use chopsticks effectively. Using chopsticks seems easy until you try it for the first time! But think of it this way. If hundreds of millions of Chinese people have been using chopsticks for every meal for over 3,000 years, then it can't be that difficult! With practice, and some patience, you can soon become an efficient "chopsticker."

Begin by following the instructions on the next page.

Although there are several different ways you can use chopsticks, the following method is perhaps the most popular:

(1) Position one chopstick in the angle between your thumb and forefinger, and, curling your third and little fingers a little toward your wrist, let it rest on the tips of the third and little finger. It is best to grasp the chopstick more than half way up from the tip. If you are holding this first chopstick correctly, it should stick in your hand without your needing to apply much pressure. You should be able to move your forefinger, your second finger, and thumb quite easily – though you won't quite be able to snap your fingers.

(2) Now for the movable chopstick. Place it between the tips of your forefinger, second finger and thumb, and hold it in whatever manner seems easiest with the pads of the two fingers and thumb. Holding the second stick as you would hold a pen is probably best.

(3) By this stage – if you have not dropped your chopsticks – the first chopstick should still be stationary, and you should be able to move the second chopstick so that the tips can pinch together, and unpinch to give a gap of about an inch. To lift pieces of food, unpinch the chopsticks, positioning one on either side of the bit of food, and then pinch the tips together, sandwiching the food in the middle. It takes practice, but you will soon learn, especially if the food is appetizing enough.

If all else fails, then use a spoon to help you. In the eyes of the Chinese, it is much worse to let good food go to waste than to be unable to use chopsticks efficiently!

Glossary

Acupuncture An ancient Chinese method of curing diseases or relieving pain in which the doctor sticks needles into special points of the body. Still much used today.

Anemic Lacking in blood and pale in a sickly way

Ancestors Grandparents, great-grandparents, great-great-grandparents, and so on; the line of people from whom one is descended.

Authentic Genuine, real.

Autonomous Having a large degree of self-government.

Collectivize To bring small units together into a larger collection.

Communists Members of the political party that claims to follow the ideas of Karl Marx, who believed that all private property should be abolished. He believed that all property should belong to the people as a whole, and everyone should work for the benefit of the wider community, and not just for themselves and their families. The Chinese Communist Party has ruled the People's Republic of China since 1949, but it has not carried out all of Marx's ideas.

Connoisseurs People with expert knowledge (of fine food, drink, art, etc.).

Conventional Expected or traditional.

Cuisine Style of cooking.

Erosion A wearing away or gradual destruction.

Focal point Center of interest.

Frugal Economical, money-saving.

Glutinous Sticky.

Gourmet An expert judge of good food.

Haute cuisine High-class style of cooking.

Incense A spice that gives off a fragrant smell when burned.

Irrigation systems Systems for channeling and supplying water to farmland.

Nutrients Units of food that provide nourishment.

Rituals Religious or traditional ceremonies.

Scholarly elite The best scholars, those who passed examinations at the highest level (and who, in traditional China, were very rich and powerful).

Staple food Main or basic food.

Steaming A cooking technique whereby bamboo steamers are piled up over a *wok* of boiling water. The steamers often have more than one tier so that several types of food may be steamed at the same time.

Stir-frying A cooking technique invented by the Cantonese. The *wok* is heated intensely and a little vegetable oil is added, plus some seasoning to flavor. Then, for a couple of minutes only, the uniformly sliced or diced ingredients are added. They are stirred and tossed, sealing in both flavor and nutrients. Control of the heat and timing is a test of the chef's skill.

Versatile Readily used in a variety of ways.

Further Reading

The Ancient Chinese by Lai Po Kan. Silver Burdett, 1985.

The Classic Chinese Cookbook by Mai Leung. Harper and Row, 1975.

Cooking the Chinese Way by Ling Yu. Lerner Publications, 1982.

A Family in China by Nance L. Fyson and Richard Greenhill.

Ken Hon's Chinese Cookery. Harper and Row, 1986.

Let's Visit China Today, revised edition, by John C. Caldwell. Harper and Row, 1973.

Take a Trip to China by Sally Mason. Franklin Watts, 1981.

Two Chinese Families by Catherine E. Sadler. Atheneum, 1981.

Picture Acknowledgments

The publishers would like to thank the following for their permission to reproduce copyright pictures: Anthony Blake 16, 27, 34; Greg Evans Photo Library *cover*, 14, 18; Sally and Richard Greenhill 10, 13, 15, 19, 21, 37; The Hutchison Library 8, 11, 20, 23, 30, 31, 32, 33, 35, 39, 40; A.I. Olley 12; Christine Osborne 25; Topham 42; Wayland Picture Library 6, 9, 29; ZEFA 38, 41. The map on page 5 is by David Noble. The map on page 7 and all step-by-step illustrations are by Juliette Nicholson.

Index

Agriculture 4, 11, 12, 13, 28
Aquaculture 14

Bean curd 15, 21, 27, 33
Beijing 6, 8, 27, 28, 33, 42

Canton 4, 25, 34, 42
Chiang Kai-shek 8
China (PRC)
    climate 4, 23, 27
    history 7–8, 9–10
    population 4, 6, 7
Chinatowns 41, 42
Chinese New Year 39
Collectivization 11–12, 13,
    19
Communism 8, 11, 39, 40
Cooking utensils
    bamboo steamers 32, 34
    chopsticks 32
    cleavers 31
    sandpots 32
    woks 31, 32
Crops 4, 10, 13, 14, 28
    rice 4, 10, 13, 14, 19, 20,
        21, 23, 25, 27, 31, 43
    wheat 4, 13, 14, 23, 28

Deng Ziaoping 12
Dim sum 33, 34
Dragon boat festival 40
Drinks 37–38
    tea 10, 14, 37–38

Emigration 6, 41

Famine 10
Fish 14, 16, 21, 23, 25, 27, 39

Fruit 14, 18, 23, 27, 30, 40
Fujian 14, 38

Guangdong 14

Hangzhou 9
Hong Kong 4, 6

Inner Mongolia 6

Manchus 7
Mao Zedong 8, 11, 12, 14
Markets 13, 18, 19
Meals 20–21, 33
Meat 9, 13, 16, 19, 20, 21,
    25, 27, 39
Mongols 7, 28
Moon Festival 39–40

National minorities 6
Noodles 18, 28, 30, 33, 42
North China Plain 4, 27

Opium 10

Pearl River Delta 4, 23, 25
Polo, Marco 9
Poultry 14, 18, 21, 25, 27,
    28, 39

Qinling Mountains 4, 13

Recipes
    Almond milk jelly 35
    Cabbage with cream
        sauce 24
    Chinese New Year cake
        40
    Fried rice 43
    Lion-heads casserole 28

Ma Po's bean curd 17
    Noodles with meat
        sauce 22
    Stir-fry chicken with
        vegetables 25
    Twice-cooked pork 26
    Wonton soup 36
Red-stewing 23, 32
Republic of China (ROC)
    6, 8
Restaurants 33–34, 35, 41,
    42

Shang Dynasty 9
Shanghai 6, 23
Sichuan 7, 27
Song Dynasty 9
Soy beans 14, 15, 33
Spices 25, 27
Steaming 23, 25, 31, 32, 34
Stir-frying 18, 23, 25, 31, 42
Stores 18, 19, 42

Taiping Rebellion 8
Taiwan 6, 7, 8, 38, 40
Tang Dynasty 9, 29
Tibet 4

Vegetables 10, 14, 16, 19,
    20, 21, 23, 25, 27, 30

Wonton 9, 34–35

Xinjiang 4
Xi River 4

Yangtze River 4, 23, 27
Yellow River 4, 28
Yuan Mei 18